25 Questions you've always wanted to ask your Muslim co-worker

Omar Jahangir

First Edition
First Printing, 2024

ISBN 978-1-0683237-0-6

For more information, inquiries, or additional resources related to this book, please visit:

Website: www.muslimcoworker.com
Email: info@muslimcoworker.com

Contents

Introduction

After finishing my studies in Physics, but before embarking on my PhD, I worked at a small engineering company as a Junior Physicist. Situated in the remote village of Tring, just on the outskirts of London, I found myself mixing with people who were predominantly white and male. Sure, there was a mix of ethnicities, some black, some South Asian, and some from the Far East. Still, the majority were those who lived within the surrounding villages. Although many had visited London, they all preferred the quiet lifestyle that a small town like Tring offered.

Tring was very different to Newham, where I grew up my whole life. The London borough of Newham houses one of the most diverse ranges of minorities within its boundaries. There are mosques, temples, churches, gurdwaras and synagogues on almost every street, with many people often wearing the traditional attire to which they belong. Tring was very different. It was quintessentially British, with a town hall where people would gather, a local pub that everyone would visit after work, and even a local marina where families could meet for weekend activities. Both places were very different.

Being visibly Muslim, with brown skin (although not all Muslims are brown), a big beard, and trousers above my ankles, I remember my first day at work was met with a curious look of interest and intrigue. Although there had been some Muslim employees within the company before I joined (I certainly wasn't the first), they often came from neighbouring villages and were accustomed to not explicitly being Muslim outside their homes.

On my first day at work, to pray the afternoon (dhuhr) prayer, I walked around looking for a door marked "prayer room", only to be told by the only other Muslim employee that the boiler-room closet is used as the prayer room. "No worries, I'm happy to pray anywhere", I said to myself.

As the weeks went by, and I started to build a rapport with my co-workers, they naturally became curious about some of the habits they had seen me doing. One time, when I took an empty water bottle to the bathroom, a co-worker proclaimed, "You don't want to be drinking the tap water in there, mate". I chuckled and responded, "Oh, thanks for the tip".

Another time during Christmas, a co-worker asked, "Do Muslims celebrate Christmas?" after handing me a thoughtful, bright red Christmas card before the holiday season.

Indeed, most of the questions within this book directly result from them asking me questions when we'd gather during lunch and tea breaks.

After leaving that role and embarking on my PhD, I interned in a research lab working on Artificial Intelligence. Again, I was surrounded by amazing people who were predominantly white male, with a few people from ethnic minorities. Again, I found myself being asked similar questions regarding Islam during lunch times by my co-workers out of genuine curiosity and interest.

Both experiences highlighted to me the need for an easy-to-read collection of popular questions that non-Muslims have regarding Islam. Indeed, Muslims only make up less than 6% of the population in the UK, and less than 2% in the US. Hence, it is no surprise that there exist people whose only exposure to Islam and Muslims is from the news and social media.

If only there was something out there that I could point my co-workers towards to answer some of the questions they had asked. Hence, the idea for this book was born.

This book is a collection of questions, some of which I have been asked directly, others I felt were pertinent to answer given the current political climate post 9/11. All are answered in the simplest way possible to provide clarity without delving too much into polemics.

So, who is this book for? Maybe you have a few Muslim co-workers and are curious about why they're always busy on a Friday afternoon. Perhaps you want to know how many times a day they pray and what that prayer looks like. Or maybe you've received this book as a gift from your Muslim co-worker. In all cases, I hope you find answers to questions you've always wanted to ask your Muslim co-worker.

1 - What do Muslims believe?

O you who believe, believe in God and His Messenger and in the Scripture He sent down to His Messenger, as well as what He sent down before. Anyone who does not believe in God, His angels, His Scriptures, His messengers, and the Last Day has gone far, far astray. (Qur'an 4:136).

Muslims believe in Allah (God) as the one and only Creator, Sustainer, and Lord of everything that exists. He is unique, without partners or equals, and alone is worthy of worship. Allah is Merciful, Just, and All-Knowing.

To guide humanity, Allah sent Prophets throughout history to teach people how to live righteous lives. These include Adam, Noah, Abraham, Moses, and Jesus, with Muhammad (peace be upon them all) as the final Prophet. All Prophets shared the same core message: to worship Allah alone and live according to His guidance.

Muslims also believe Allah revealed divine scriptures to certain Prophets as guidance for their people. The most well-known include the Torah given to Moses, the Bible (Injeel) given to Jesus, and the Qur'an, revealed to Muhammad (peace be upon them all), which Muslims believe is the final, unchanged word of God.

As a sign of their truthfulness, Allah granted Prophets miracles, events beyond human capacity, as proof of their prophethood. These include the parting of the sea for Moses, the healing of the blind and the leper for Jesus, and the splitting of the Moon for Muhammad (peace be upon them all).

In addition, Muslims hold six key beliefs:

1. Belief in Allah.
2. Belief in angels.
3. Belief in divine scriptures.
4. Belief in Prophets.
5. Belief in the Day of Judgment.
6. Belief in Divine Decree (Qadr), while
acknowledging human free will.

Together, these beliefs form the foundation
of a Muslim's faith and worldview. Islam
emphasizes the oneness of God, the unity of
humanity, and the importance of living a
moral and purposeful life in preparation for
the Hereafter.

2 - How many times a day do Muslims pray?

Indeed, prayer has been decreed upon the believers at appointed times. (Qur'an 4:103).

Muslims pray five times a day, split evenly throughout. These are:
- Dawn (Fajr)
- Afternoon (Dhuhr)
- Late-afternoon (Asr)
- After Sunset (Maghrib)
- Evening Prayer (Isha)

The prayers can be held in congregation or by oneself, with no fixed timing for its duration. The time taken depends on how much time one has to devote to the prayer, with as little as five minutes being sufficient for those with limited time.

Having prayers spread throughout the day

allows Muslims to clear their minds of all the troubles and stresses that a typical day brings while constantly reminding Muslims of a higher goal in life.

Islamic prayer is an intimate conversation between God and His servants; hence, it is an integral part of Islam. Extra prayers are encouraged immediately before or after these prayers and at other times during the day. An emphasis is also given to voluntary prayers in the latter portion of the night.

3 - Why do Muslims fast during Ramadan?

O believers! Fasting is prescribed for you - as it was for those before you, so perhaps you will become mindful of Allah. (Qur'an 2:183)

Muslims fast for 30 days each year during

the Islamic month of Ramadan. The fast
begins at dawn and ends at sunset daily, with
its duration varying based on the time of
year. While fasting, Muslims abstain from
eating, drinking, and marital intimacy,
focusing on maintaining good character and
treating others with kindness.

Fasting during Ramadan is a fundamental
obligation for Muslims, similar to the
requirement of praying the five daily
prayers. It is an act of worship prescribed by
God and one of the Five Pillars of Islam,
emphasizing devotion and submission to
God.

In addition to fulfilling this obligation,
fasting serves to nurture the soul through
increased prayers and acts of service. It is
also a means to develop self-discipline and
break bad habits. By refraining from food
and drink, individuals gain greater control

over their desires, which can help them overcome other vices.

The month concludes with the celebration of Eid ul-Fitr, a joyous festival where Muslims gather with family and friends to mark the end of fasting, congratulating one another on completing this spiritual journey. Certain individuals are exempt from fasting during the month due to its physical demands, including the elderly, the sick, children, menstruating women, and those who are pregnant.

4 - What exactly is Halal?

So eat from the good, lawful things which Allah has provided for you, and be grateful for Allah's favours, if you truly worship Him alone. (Qur'an 16:114)

Halal, is an Arabic word which means

"permissible," and defines what is lawful in Islam. For meat and poultry, this means the animal must be slaughtered in a specific way, with the name of Allah being mentioned during the slaughter, in order to make it suitable for consumption.

5 - Why don't Muslims drink Alcohol?

O you who believe! Wine, gambling, idolatrous practices and divining arrows are filth, made up by Satan. Therefore, refrain from it, so that you may be successful. (Qur'an 5:90)

Alcohol and drugs are known to impair the senses and disrupt the faculty to think. How many times do people who drink too much act in a manner which can often be dangerous to not just themselves but others, too? Hence, Islam has prohibited the consumption of intoxicants.

6 - Why don't Muslims eat pork?

He has only forbidden to you dead animals, blood, the flesh of swine, and that which has been dedicated to other than Allah. (Qur'an 2:173)

Muslims refrain from consuming pork due to clear prohibitions outlined in the Qur'an. This prohibition is mentioned in several verses, often alongside other forbidden items such as carrion and blood.

Although the Qur'an does not explicitly provide the rationale, various interpretations and scholarly explanations have emerged throughout Islamic history. One prominent explanation is that pigs are regarded as impure animals, and in Islam, what we consume is believed to impact both our physical health and spiritual well-being.

Therefore, only that which is pure and

wholesome has been made permissible
(Halal) for Muslims to consume.

7 - Who was Muhammad (pbuh)? Why do Muslims get so upset regarding his depictions?

And We have not sent you, [O Muḥammad], except as a mercy to the worlds. (Qur'an 21:107)

The Prophet Muhammad (peace be upon him) was the last Prophet to be sent by God as guidance for humanity. He lived approximately 1400 years ago, with Muslims believing that the Archangel Gabriel (peace be upon him) delivered revelation from God to the Prophet Muhammad (peace be upon him) over a period of 23 years. This revelation was collated and written into a book form, The Qur'an, and has been preserved word-for-word since then.

Although there are numerous written descriptions of the Prophet Muhammad's (peace be upon him) physical features, Muslims refrain from depicting these in image form out of reverence and respect.

Also, since none of his companions drew pictures of him, any images displayed would not be accurate and, hence, misleading and also considered to be offensive.

This principle extends to all prophets in Islam, including Jesus, Moses, Abraham, and others (peace be upon them all). Depicting any prophet is regarded as deeply disrespectful and profoundly hurtful to Muslims, as it diminishes the reverence and honor bestowed upon them by God.

8 - What happens inside a mosque?

*The mosques of Allāh are only to be maintained by
those who believe in Allāh and the Last Day and
establish prayer and give zakāh and do not fear
except Allāh, for it is expected that those will be of
the [rightly] guided.* (Qur'an 9:18)

A mosque, also known as a Masjid, is a place
where Muslims gather for worship. An
announcement will be made for the call to
prayer (known as the Adhan). Thereafter, the
person leading the prayer (the Imam) will
lead the congregation. This occurs for each
of the five daily prayers.

At other times, the Mosque serves as the
central hub for Muslims in the locality,
offering services such as marriage
counselling, funeral processing and youth
engagement.

Islamic education, known as Madrasah, is often provided for young children to help them learn about their religion, with additional services and programs available for adults as well.

Mosques also play a significant role in fostering community cohesion. Many now host open days, inviting local non-Muslims to visit, engage, and learn more about Islam.

9 - Why are Muslims always busy on Friday afternoons?

O you who believe, when the call for Salāh (prayer) is proclaimed on Friday, hasten for the remembrance of God, and leave off business. That is much better for you, if only you knew. (Qur'an 62:9)

Friday, known as the Day of Jumu'ah, holds

special significance in Islam, as it includes a mandatory congregational prayer for all eligible males. This prayer replaces the regular Dhuhr (Afternoon) prayer on Fridays and must be performed in congregation.

A key feature of the Jumu'ah prayer is the sermon, or khutbah, delivered by the Imam. The sermon provides guidance and reminds the congregation of the virtuous teachings and principles of Islam.

While it is not obligatory for women and children to attend, they are welcome to participate in the prayer if they so wish.

10 - What is Hajj?

The Hajj [pilgrimage] takes place during the prescribed months. Then there should be no indecent speech, misbehaviour, or quarrelling for anyone

Hajj is the annual pilgrimage that takes place in Makkah, Saudi Arabia, and is one of the most significant acts of worship in Islam. It is a mandatory religious duty for every Muslim who is physically and financially capable to undertake at least once in their lifetime.

During Hajj, millions of Muslims from all over the world - often exceeding 3 million people - gather to perform a series of sacred rituals. These rituals commemorate the actions of the Prophet Ibrahim (Abraham), his wife Hajar, and their son Isma'il (Ishmael), emphasizing themes of devotion, sacrifice, and unity.

A unique aspect of Hajj is the attire. Men wear two simple, white, unstitched garments known as Ihram, symbolizing purity, humility, and equality before God, as no distinctions of wealth or status are visible.

While there is no specific uniform for women, they are required to dress modestly in accordance with Islamic guidelines. Both men and women are expected to uphold the highest standards of behavior during Hajj, including patience, kindness, and humility.

Hajj is not only a deeply spiritual journey but also a powerful symbol of Muslim unity. Millions stand together in worship of The One True God; transcending differences of nationality, ethnicity, and social status.

At the conclusion of Hajj, Muslims around the world celebrate Eid al-Adha, also known as the Festival of Sacrifice. The celebration is marked by communal prayers, feasts, acts of charity, and the ritual sacrifice of an animal, with the meat shared among family, friends, and those in need.

Alongside Hajj, Muslims also perform Umrah, an additional pilgrimage that can be undertaken at any time of the year. While not mandatory, Umrah holds great spiritual significance and involves some of the same rituals as Hajj, such as wearing the Ihram and performing Tawaf (circling the Kaaba). It is referred to as the "minor pilgrimage" and is a recommended act of worship for those who are able to undertake it.

11 - Why do you wash your feet in the sink?

O you who believe, when you rise to [perform] prayer, wash your faces and your forearms to the elbows and wipe over your heads and wash your feet up to the ankles. (Qur'an 5:6).

Before performing prayer, Muslims must ensure they are in a state of cleanliness through a ritual washing called Wudhu (ablution). This process involves washing specific parts of the body, including the face, hands, arms, and feet.

So, if you ever notice a Muslim co-worker washing their feet in the sink, it simply means they are completing the final step of this purification process.

12 - Why do I see some Muslims taking a water bottle when they go to the bathroom?

Indeed God loves those who constantly repent and loves those who purify themselves. (Qur'an 2:222).

Islam places great importance on cleanliness and personal hygiene. So, if you notice your

Muslim co-worker taking a water bottle to the bathroom, it's likely being used for washing and cleansing themselves as part of their hygiene practices after using the restroom.

A follow-up to this question is that, when visiting a Muslim family's home, you may notice a watering-can like container in the bathroom. This watering-can is what Muslims would use to clean themselves after using the toilet. They come in various shapes and sizes, depending on preference.

13 - Why do some Muslim men have their trousers above their ankles?

Indeed, in the Messenger of Allah you have an excellent example for whoever has hope in Allah and the Last Day, and remembers Allah often. (Qur'an 33:21).

Some Muslim males may be seen as keeping their trousers above their ankles. This action was the practice of the Prophet Muhammad (peace be upon him), who thus encouraged males to do so as a sign of humbleness and humility.

Muslims are encouraged to follow the practice of the Prophet Muhammad (peace be upon him) in all aspects of their lives, as he is considered the perfect role model for mankind.

14 - Why do so many Muslim men have beards?

Similar to answer 13, Muslims try to follow the teachings of the Prophet Muhammad (peace be upon him) as much as possible. One of his teachings was to encourage males to grow their beard.

Throughout history, distinguished males had beards, as it was seen as a sign of nobility. Although this trend has changed in recent times, Muslims are still encouraged to keep one.

15 - What is the role of Women in Islam? Does Islam prevent women from getting an education?

To whoever, male or female, does good deeds and has faith, We shall give a good life and reward them according to the best of their actions.
(Qur'an 16:97)

Women are considered equal to men in Islam. However, there are differences in their roles and responsibilities in society and family life. In Islam, men and women have different but complementary roles, and both are valued and respected. Women have a

right to education, work, and property
ownership, just like men.

Islam encourages learning knowledge, with
the Prophet Muhammad (peace be upon
him) stating that learning the fundamentals
of faith is incumbent on everyone, males and
females alike.

The first university in the world was
established by a Muslim woman, Fatima bint
Muhammad Al-Fihriya, in the city of Fez,
Morocco, in 859 CE. This institution, known
as the University of Al-Qarawiyyin,
continues to symbolize the deep Islamic
tradition of valuing education and
empowering individuals through knowledge.

16 - Why do I sometimes see Muslim women covering their hair? Are they forced to do that?

In Islam, women past the age of puberty are required to cover their bodies, including their hair, as obligated by God. By doing so, they are outwardly manifesting their submission to God's commands and pursuit of His pleasure. His commands here have personal and societal benefit including protecting women from unwanted attention. Depending on culture, the headscarf (also called Hijab) can be worn differently, with new trends constantly evolving.

Other orthodox Muslims may prefer to cover their face too, hence they would wear the Burqa (or Niqab), with only male members whom they are related to being able to see them without it. These include husbands, sons, fathers, brothers etc.

The large majority of Muslim women who either wear the Hijab or Burqa do so out of their own choice. It allows them to feel empowered by restricting and preserving their sexuality and beauty only for their spouse, whilst also expressing their commitment to God by following His commands.

17 - Why don't some Muslim women shake hands with males, and vice-versa?

In Islam, physical contact between men and women who are not related to each other is prohibited. This includes actions like shaking hands.

The prohibition is rooted in Islamic principles of maintaining physical modesty and avoiding situations that could lead to discomfort or misunderstanding.

For many Muslims, this choice is not about disrespect or rejection but rather a personal religious commitment. Just as some people might decline a handshake for cultural, health, or personal reasons, Muslims who avoid shaking hands with the opposite gender do so out of devotion to their faith.

18 - Can a woman be an Imam?

The word Imam means someone who is in front and generally relates to the one who leads the five daily prayers. As Islam emphasises protecting the modesty of women, if a woman were to be an Imam to men, seeing a woman prostrate in front would lead the majority of men to be distracted easily. This is one reason a woman cannot be an Imam in a congregation of men. However, women are allowed to lead if the congregation consists only of women.

19 - How do Muslims bury their deceased? Do they cremate them?

From the Earth We created you, and into it We will return you, and from it We will bring you back again. (Qur'an, 20:55)

Cremation is not permitted in Islam. When a Muslim passes away, they are buried in the ground in accordance with Islamic traditions. Men are shrouded in three white garments, while women are shrouded in five white garments. Before burial, the deceased is carefully washed in a ritual bath to purify them. Following this, relatives and members of the community gather to offer the Janazah (funeral) prayer, seeking forgiveness and mercy for the departed.

The burial itself is simple, with the body placed directly into the grave facing the Qibla (the direction of Makkah).

While coffins may be used to transport the body from the hospital or home to the graveyard, the deceased is traditionally not buried in the coffin. Instead, the body is placed directly into the grave, following the Islamic practice of returning to the earth in simplicity and humility.

20 - Do Muslims celebrate Easter or Christmas?

Muslims believe that Jesus (peace be upon him) was a Prophet of God and was born to the Virgin Mary (peace be upon her). Muslims also believe that Jesus (peace be upon him) will return nearer the end of times.

The main difference is that Muslims do not believe Jesus (peace be upon him) was crucified, with the Qur'an being very clear regarding this:

And they did not kill him, nor did they crucify him, but [another] was made to resemble him to them.
(Qur'an, 4:157)

Thus, the Qur'an makes it very clear in rejecting statements regarding the crucifixion of Jesus (may peace be upon him). Due to this, Muslims do not believe in or celebrate Easter.

As for Christmas, Muslims do not celebrate the birth of Jesus (peace be upon him), as it is unknown when the birth of Jesus (peace be upon him) took place. As such, Muslims do not partake in Christmas celebrations.

21 - Why is the Qur'an a miracle?

This is the Book about which there is no doubt, a guidance for those conscious of Allah. (Qur'an, 2:2)

It is not possible for this Quran to have been produced by anyone other than Allah. In fact, it is a confirmation of what came before, and an explanation of the [former] Scripture. It is, without a doubt, from the Lord of all the worlds.
(Qur'an, 10:37)

The Qur'an is the holy book of Islam, believed by Muslims to be the literal word of God as revealed to the Prophet Muhammad (peace be upon him) through the Angel Gabriel over a period of 23 years. It serves as the primary source of guidance for Muslims, covering all aspects of life, including spirituality, morality, law, and personal conduct.

It is divided into 114 chapters, called surahs, which vary in length and address themes such as the oneness of God, stories of earlier prophets, ethical principles, and the purpose of life.

There are many reasons why the Qur'an is considered a miracle, three of which will be mentioned here. Firstly, it is due to the eloquence of the speech within the Qur'an. Having been sent to the Prophet Muhammad (peace be upon him), who was not able to read or write and was not known for his poetry, the Qur'an was able to provide such eloquence in the manner and style with which it addressed mankind. So much so that it challenged anyone to bring forth even a similar chapter, yet no one has been able to do so.

Secondly, the Qur'an provides information that would be impossible for the Prophet

Muhammad (peace be upon him) to have known, as he was illiterate and thus unable to read or write. Incidents relating to the previous prophets, such as Abraham, Moses and Jesus, are mentioned. Yet, those incidents were reserved for those who were able to read and write and from the Jews and Christians at the time.

Thirdly, it describes phenomena which were impossible to know approximately 1400 years ago. These range from the development of the foetus to the physical make-up of human beings from water and the movements of the celestial bodies in space.

22 - What is the difference between Sunni and Shia Islam?

After the Prophet Muhammad (peace be

upon him) passed away in 632 CE, one of his closest companions, Abu Bakr (may God be pleased with him), was selected as the leader of the Muslim community, earning the title of Caliph (successor). Sunnis believe this was the correct decision, as they interpret the Prophet's appointment of Abu Bakr to lead prayers in his absence as a sign of his suitability to lead the Muslim community after the Prophet.

On the other hand, Shias hold that leadership should have passed to Ali (may God be pleased with him), the cousin and son-in-law of the Prophet Muhammad (peace be upon him), whom they believe was divinely designated as the rightful successor.

The division between Sunnis and Shias marks the emergence of two main branches of Islam following the Prophet's (peace be upon him) death. While both share core tenets of faith, such as belief in the Qur'an and the Prophethood of Muhammad (peace be upon him), there are differences in beliefs, religious practices, leadership structures, and interpretations of Islamic law between the two groups.

23 - What does Jihad mean?

Fight in the way of Allāh those who fight against you but do not transgress. Indeed, Allāh does not like transgressors. (Qur'an 2:197)

"Jihad" is an Arabic term that means "to struggle" or "to strive." In Islam, it can refer to a spiritual struggle that one may undergo to become a better Muslim or a physical struggle to defend oneself or one's community. The latter is often referred to as "physical *Jihad*" and is only permissible in certain circumstances, such as when a

Muslim country is under attack.

And even in this scenario, Islam mandates that strict ethical guidelines must be followed. Civilians, non-combatants, women, children, the elderly, and religious clergy are not to be harmed. Places of worship, crops, and infrastructure must also be protected. Additionally, prisoners of war must be treated with dignity and provided food and shelter. The Prophet Muhammad (peace be upon him) is reported to have instructed:

"Do not kill women, children, the elderly, or those who are not fighting."

The Prophet Muhammad (peace be upon him) referred to the internal struggle one may go through as the best form of *"Jihad"*, detailing how working on oneself is paramount to Islam.

Islam is not inherently violent. It is a holistic way of life that governs everything a Muslim does to please God. The vast majority of Muslims are peaceful, and follow the religion's teachings of peace, tolerance, and respect for all people. However, there have been instances of violence carried out in the name of Islam. This violence is often motivated by political, social, or economic factors rather than by religious ideology.

It is important to recognize that any religion or ideology has the potential to be misused as a tool for violence. This is because such systems can provide a strong sense of identity and purpose, which can be exploited to mobilize people for political or social objectives. Furthermore, they may be manipulated to justify violence by framing certain groups as enemies or threats.

24 - What is Islam's view on the LGBTQ+ community?

The Muslim belief is that it is not permissible to act upon the urges resulting from homosexual thoughts and feelings, as they go against the teachings of Islam. Acting upon such thoughts will lead a Muslim to be sinful. Believing that such actions are lawful and permissible for Muslims is more severe and will lead a person to leave the religion of Islam.

However, it must be stressed that whilst Muslims consider acts of homosexuality to be impermissible for those adhering to Islam (i.e. Muslims), for those choosing to live a different lifestyle where homosexuality is permissible, Muslims must treat them with respect and tolerence, just as they would anyone else.

Gender reassignment therapy is not something that Islam permits due to it being a form of changing the creation of God.

25 - What is Sharia law?

O you who believe, uphold justice and bear witness to God, even if it is against yourselves, your parents, or your close relatives. Whether the person is rich or poor, God is more worthy of both.
Refrain from following your own desire, so that you can act justly- if you distort or neglect justice, God is fully aware of what you do. (Qur'an 4:135)

Sharia, or Islamic law, is the law derived from the Qur'an and the statements of the Prophet Muhammad (peace be upon him). It covers everything about the day-to-day activities of Muslims, including aspects such as business transactions, personal relationships, inheritance, prayer, and cleanliness. The essence of Sharia law is to guide people on how to best live their lives in a way that is most loved by God.

The beauty of these laws and the way Muslims interacted with other peoples during the late 7th and 8th centuries until now has allowed people to see the beauty of Islam and accept the religion.

This has led to Islam becoming the fastest growing religion in the world today, with people from different backgrounds, ethnicities and beliefs accepting Islam and becoming Muslim.

Final remarks

In writing this book, I discovered that many of the questions people have about Islam and Muslims often center around one fundamental question: why would someone choose to be a Muslim? Why would anyone willingly restrict their diet by avoiding alcohol and pork? Why would a woman choose to wear the Hijab in a world that celebrates open expression of sexuality? Why commit to praying five times a day, even at what may seem like inconvenient times?

The answer to these questions, and so many more, lies in one simple truth: a Muslim's life revolves entirely around God. Every action, whether waking up, going to work, eating and drinking, spending time with family, praying, fasting, or even resting, is undertaken with the intention of pleasing God. To be a Muslim means to submit wholeheartedly to the will of God, finding purpose and fulfillment in living a life aligned with His guidance.

But who is this God, this Allah, to whom Muslims submit so devoutly? The Qur'an provides a beautiful description:

"He is Allāh, other than whom there is no deity, Knower of the unseen and the witnessed. He is the Entirely Merciful, the Especially Merciful.

He is Allāh, other than whom there is no deity, the Sovereign, the Pure, the Perfection, the Grantor of Security, the Overseer, the Exalted in Might, the Compeller, the Superior. Exalted is Allāh above whatever they associate with Him.

He is Allāh, the Creator, the Producer, the Fashioner; to Him belong the best names. Whatever is in the heavens and earth is exalting Him. And He is the Exalted in Might, the Wise." - (Qur'an 59:22-24)

The ultimate aim of a Muslim's life is to worship God and live in a way that pleases Him, striving to embody kindness, justice, and humility.

Muslims view life as a test - a temporary journey where deeds, intentions, and actions determine their standing in the eternal life to come. Allah reminds us in the Qur'an:

"And this worldly life is nothing but amusement and diversion; but the Hereafter is better for those who are mindful of Allah. So will you not reason?"
(Qur'an 6:32).

This perspective helps Muslims stay grounded, knowing that the trials and blessings of this world are fleeting, and true success lies in attaining God's mercy and the eternal paradise He has prepared.

If reading this book has sparked your

curiosity or inspired you to learn more about Islam, I warmly encourage you to explore further. Islam is a faith of simplicity, profound spirituality, and purpose; offering guidance for every aspect of life.

Whether through speaking to a Muslim colleague, visiting a local mosque, reading the Qur'an, or learning about the life of the Prophet Muhammad (peace be upon him), there are many ways to learn about Islam.

I pray that you found this book informative and engaging, and helped answer the most pertinent questions you have had regarding Muslims and Islam.

If you have any additional questions or would like to learn more, please feel free to visit www.muslimcoworker.com or email info@muslimcoworker.com for more information.

Glossary of commonly used words and phrases.

Adhan: Call to prayer.

Ameen: An Arabic expression said after making a supplication.

Allah: The Arabic name for God in Islam.

Allahu Akbar: *"Allah is the Greatest,"* a common Islamic phrase.

Barakah: Blessings or divine goodness.

Bismillah: *"In the name of Allah,"* often said before beginning any task.

Dawah: Invitation to Islam or sharing Islamic teachings.

Dhikr: Remembrance of Allah.

Dua: Supplication or prayer.

Eid: Festive celebrations, particularly Eid ul-Fitr and Eid ul-Adha.

Fiqh: Islamic jurisprudence or understanding.

Fitnah: Trials or tribulations.

Hajj: Pilgrimage to Makkah, obligatory for

Muslims who can afford it.

Halal: Permissible or lawful in Islam.

Haram: Prohibited or forbidden in Islam.

Hijab: Modest clothing, particularly headscarf worn by Muslim women.

Iftar: Breaking the fast during Ramadan.

Imam: Prayer leader or spiritual guide.

Insha'Allah: *"If Allah wills,"* used to express hope for the future.

Islam: The religion founded on the teachings of Prophet Muhammad (peace be upon him).

Janazah: Islamic Funeral Prayer.

Jannah: Paradise.

Jummah: Friday, the day of congregational prayer.

Khutbah: Sermon delivered during Friday prayers.

Madrasah: Islamic school or educational institution.

Mahram: Unmarriageable kin with whom marriage is forbidden.

Masha'Allah: An Arabic phrase expressing appreciation or admiration.

Masjid: Mosque or Islamic place of worship.

Mubarak: Blessed or happy.

Mufti: Islamic scholar qualified to issue legal opinions.

Muslim: A follower of the Islamic faith.

Nikah: Islamic marriage ceremony.

Qadr: Divine destiny or preordainment.

Qibla: Direction towards the Kaaba in Makkah, faced during prayer.

Qur'an: Holy book of Islam.

Ramadan: Month of fasting in the Islamic calendar.

Sadaqah: Voluntary charitable giving.

Sadaqah Jariyah: Continuous charity.

Salah (Salat): Ritual prayer performed by Muslims.

Shahada: The Islamic declaration of faith.

Sharia: Islamic law derived from the Quran and Hadith.

Shia: One of the major branches of Islam.

Shirk: Associating partners with Allah, considered a major sin.

Suhoor: Pre-dawn meal before fasting begins.

Sunnah: The practices and traditions of Prophet Muhammad.

Sunni: Another major branch of Islam.

Surah: A chapter in the Qur'an.

Tafsir: Exegesis or commentary on the Qur'an.

Tahajjud: Night prayer performed during the last third of the night.

Takbir: The phrase "Allahu Akbar," often said in specific situations or during rituals.

Taqwa: Consciousness of God, piety.

Tawakkul: Trust in Allah's plan.

Tawheed: Oneness of God.

Umrah: Voluntary pilgrimage to Makkah.

Ummah: The global Muslim community.

Wudhu: Ritual washing before prayer.

Zakat: Obligatory almsgiving or charity.